W9-CMP-732

Christmas
in
Colonial and Early America

The modern-day artist J. L. G. Ferris conjures up this
nostalgic view of Philadelphia on Christmas Eve in 1773.

Christmas
in
Colonial and Early America

Christmas Around the World
From World Book

World Book, Inc.
a Scott Fetzer company

Chicago London Sydney Toronto

World Book, Inc.
525 W. Monroe
Chicago, IL 60661

For information on other World Book products, call 1-800-255-1750, x3771.

ISBN: 0-7166-0875-8
LC: 96-60210

Printed in Mexico.

2 3 4 5 6 7 8 9 10 99 98 97 96

Contents

Introduction   7

Christmas in the Colonies   9

A Christmas Collection of Toys   24

Carrying Christmas Throughout the Land   28

Early American Decorations   38

Christmas with the First Family   43

The Evolution of Santa Claus   47

A Victorian Christmas   52

Season's Greetings   63

A Christmas Sampler   65

Index   78

Introduction

Christmas is a time of the spirit. The men and women of Colonial and early America kept the Christmas spirit alive, often under the most difficult circumstances. The desperate soldiers of the Continental Army under General George Washington spent their Christmas Eve of 1776 preparing a blow for liberty that saved a young nation. On the trail, as pioneers opened up a vast new continent, they would keep a simple Christmas with whatever they could find. Perhaps it would be just a lonely miner rapping on a tin plate with a spoon to make a little holiday noise or a young child from a sodbuster community on the prairie getting a single sack of candy. But it was Christmas and they celebrated as best they could. The religious services and holiday customs came from every country in Europe as streams of immigrants landed in a new land, bringing their hopes with them. The spirit of good cheer in times when there seems to be very little to be cheerful about is part of the most priceless heritage our forefathers have left to us. And it is that spirit we wish to celebrate in this book.

There are many illustrations in this volume. We have used photographs of historic sites, paintings, lithographs, and drawings. Wherever possible, we have gone back to the original art work of the period to illustrate our story. But those hard-working Americans in the early days of our country were often too busy making history to stop to record it. Several of the illustrations in this book were drawn or painted at a later time. They are all as accurate as artists are likely to be when recalling the nostalgic days of the past.

Merry Christmas
The Editors

The Governor's Palace in Williamsburg, Virginia

Christmas in the Colonies

For the first Christmas in the New World we have to go all the way back to the initial voyage of Christopher Columbus in 1492. His expedition of three small vessels had first sighted land on October 12. He and his men spent the next two and a half months exploring the strange new islands they assumed were part of the Indies. On the morning of Christmas Day, Columbus' flagship, the *Santa Maria*, went aground off Hispaniola.

The explorer took this accident as a sign from God that he wanted the voyagers to start a colony on that spot. With timbers from the *Santa Maria*, the crew built a fortified camp which Columbus christened *Villa de la Navidad*, or Town of the Nativity. It was the first European attempt to settle in the New World since Vikings had tried to found a settlement in Newfoundland almost five hundred years earlier. The Navidad colony failed as the Viking colony had, but, as before, other Europeans would follow.

Jamestown Colony in Virginia is thought to have been the site of the first Christmas in North America, in 1607. The English had made two previous attempts to create a permanent colony, one in Newfoundland and one on Roanoke Island. Both had ended in death and disastrous failure. On Christmas Day of 1607 it did not seem that Jamestown would succeed, either. Of the slightly more than 100 pioneers who had settled on the marshy banks of the James River in Virginia the previous May, only thirty-eight were left alive. The rest were dead from famine, malaria, and attacks by Native Americans.

The small band of survivors was ready to abandon the colony, but even in their discouragement and misery, they took the time to hold a simple Christmas service. Even as they prayed, the supply vessels bringing relief were on their way and for the first time in American history a colony was established which would grow and thrive.

One hundred and sixty-nine years later one further historic event was to take place on Christmas—when George Washington crossed the Delaware and took the British enemy by surprise, an important turning point in the American Revolution.

Is it any wonder that Americans celebrate Christmas with a special joy?

Early colonists and the thousands of brave settlers who followed them created a new land of diverse customs. These seekers of opportunity and freedom came from all over Europe. And just as they brought the tools of their trades, they brought their own ways of observing Christmas.

Compared to the jubilant ways with which we keep Christmas today, however, some of the early colonial practices were something less than convivial. The Pilgrims of Plymouth Colony in Massachusetts, founded in 1620, reflected their faith's stern edict against what were called "Bacchanalian Christmases." For the Pilgrims, the first December 25 in America was just one more day of work.

A model of Columbus' flagship the *Santa Maria*

Washington and his tattered army cross the Delaware
River on Christmas Night of 1776 to attack Trenton.

A few daring souls attempted to make merry the following
Christmas, claiming that to work would be against their con-
sciences. Governor Bradford retorted that "it was against his
conscience that they should play & others work. If they made ye
keeping of it a matter of devotion, let them keepe their houses,
but there should be no gaming or revelling in ye streets."

The Pilgrims belonged to the Puritan sect of the Church of
England, and had left their mother country to sail to the New
World where, they hoped, they could practice their beliefs in
their own way. As their name implies, the Puritans were de-
termined to lead lives that were "pure" of anything which was
not specifically written down in the Bible. And the Bible made
no mention of Christmas parties or celebrations. In Puritan
eyes, Christmas was not only immoral but illegal as well. Even
mince pies were outlawed.

A decree issued in 1659 formally banned the observance of
Christmas—and all other like holidays—with a penalty of five

shillings to be levied against any lawbreaker. Although the decree itself was repealed in 1681, the Puritan clergymen kept up their opposition in fiery sermons. For his Christmas Day service in 1712, the brimstone-sniffing minister Cotton Mather lashed out at his congregation saying, "Can you in your conscience think that our Holy Saviour is honored by Mad Mirth, by long Eating, by hard Drinking, by lewd Gaming, by rude Revelling? . . . If you will yet go on and will do Such Things, I forewarn you That the Burning Wrath of God will break forth among you."

Christmas in the Colonial era of Virginia was something else, however. There, Christmas was not simply another day but a long, rollicking season. For landowners, the holiday season was a natural extension of rural life in Virginia. The fall plowing was done, crops were harvested, and the tobacco was gathered and stored.

It was time to celebrate. The great homes of the wealthy were thrown open and guests came and went as they pleased. No one bothered with invitations, and a Virginia hostess had no idea how many guests she might expect for dinner—or to spend the night—or even a few weeks. In 1746, a London magazine declared, "All over the Colony, an universal Hospitality reigns." And despite a nose-in-the-air comment from the aristocratic Thomas Jefferson that their activities showed them to be "in a state of deplorable barbarism," Virginians enjoyed themselves immensely.

By day the men rode to hounds or hunted the plentiful game—turkeys, ducks, pigeons, and geese—that abounded. At night, parties were made merry by music, dancing, and games that often went on until nearly dawn. Philip Fithian, a young divinity student from Princeton University who served as a tutor for the offspring of the wealthy planter, Robert Carter, has left us one of the few early accounts of a Virginia Christmas party.

Carter's lands sprawled over 75,000 acres of countryside, and he could well afford to offer lavish entertainment. After breakfast—parties in Virginia started early in those days—Mr. Fithian tells of entering a large ballroom and seeing "several Minuets danced with great ease and propriety; after which the whole company Joined in country dances, and it was indeed beautiful to admiration to see such a number of young persons, set off by dress to the best advantage, moving easily to the sound of well performed Music, and with perfect regularity, tho' apparently in the utmost disorder. The Dance continued til two, we dined at half after three—soon after dinner we repaired to the Dancing-Room again. . . . When it grew too dark to dance, the young gentlemen walked over to my room and we conversed til half after six." Meanwhile the great hall was lit with hundreds of candles, and "looked luminous and splendid." Everyone then returned for more dancing and parlor games until supper was served.

Although the good squires of Virginia were mostly English born, as were the Puritans of the North, they chose to re-create the merry Christmas customs of Medieval England as best they

For the Puritans *(above)* Christmas was just another day. But Colonial Dutch children *(above right)* celebrated the arrival of *Sinterklaas* by putting out wooden shoes for him to fill. The prosperous Dutch settlers of New York *(below right)* shut down their businesses and enjoyed themselves for a whole month.

could. No Puritan asceticism for them. The Yule log, usually of oak and of immense size, was cut in the forest, hauled to the house, and set afire on the hearth. Originally a Norse custom, the burning of the Yule log was adopted by the English many centuries ago. Among other superstitions, it was thought to bring good luck to the house for the year to come. Masses of holly, fir, and mistletoe decorated doors, halls, and ballrooms.

Virginia was a land of huge plantations and the affluent owners were expected to be generous with their tenants and the poor in general. Servants and slaves were given Christmas presents, and unless they were needed for the great parties, they were given the season off.

While the Christmas celebration was largely of English derivation, Virginia's Christmas Day began with an American accent.

The country squires of Virginia liked to celebrate the Christmas season in high style. This elegant holiday setting is in the Governor's Palace in historic Williamsburg.

14

On the morning of the 25th, a great roar would resound throughout the countryside as every man fired off his musket to announce the start of the big day. Strings of firecrackers were set off, cannons would boom out a salute, and if a man had nothing else to make noise with, he would set up a clatter with pots and pans from the kitchen. This noisemaking became a tradition throughout the South.

Religious services, if any, were generally brief. As did most people in those days, Virginians read their Bibles daily. They knew what day it was.

The next major event of the day was dinner. A Virginia Christmas repast might well extend to seven or eight courses. That prestigious landowner, George Washington, set a holiday table typical of the era. Turtle soup, oysters, crab, codfish, roast beef and Yorkshire pudding, venison, boiled mutton, suckling pig, and hickory smoked ham were most likely served, along with a roast turkey. With stuffing. At least five vegetables, hot biscuits and cornbread, and a variety of relishes followed. For dessert there were often as many as a dozen choices—pies, tarts, puddings, cakes, ice cream, and fruit. And so that no one could possibly complain of hunger, dishes of nuts, raisins, and candy rounded out the impressive display.

Christmas had a special significance for George Washington and his wife, Martha. They were married in 1759 on January 6, Twelfth Night, the traditional last fling of the Christmas season. Most of us now tend to think of Washington as the legendary father of his country, and a rather solemn-faced figure on the dollar bill. But to his friends in Virginia he was known as a magnificent horseman who rode "with ease, elegance and power" and one of the most gracious hosts in the Old Dominion. A dinner or supper at the Washingtons' was the high point of any Virginian's Christmas season.

An old Virginia saying claimed if you lost all of your senses except that of smell you would still know when it was Christmas. Certainly the kitchen at Mount Vernon poured forth a wealth of glorious odors...mince pies, fruit cakes, plum puddings. "The joyous fumes of Christmas," they were once called.

The traditionally English wassail bowl, a punch of spiced wine or ale with apples, was usually offered at some point in the festivities, as well as port and Madeira. In addition, genial host

A busy Christmas kitchen in Williamsburg. A huge feast
for the guests meant a lot of work for the servants.

Washington enjoyed concocting a particularly potent eggnog
from his own recipe, which was always popular among the most
iron-stomached of his guests.

Although gift-giving to tenants and servants was considered
obligatory, the idea of bestowing heaps of presents upon friends
and members of the family at Christmas did not come to the
South until well into the next century. A kiss and a small toy
were usually the limit of parental affection for children; for
friends best wishes for the new year were considered sufficient.
But George Washington was an indulgent father and an excep-
tion to the rule, as witnessed by an extensive list of Christmas
presents for his two stepchildren he made in 1759 (left).

Sadly, the happy observances of Christmas were shortly forced
to halt for a time. The American dream of a free New World was
in trouble. Thirteen colonies had been established along the
coast of North America. Angered by heavy taxes and interfer-
ence by England, they had declared their independence from the
Crown. Winning that independence was not so simple. George
Washington had left his comfortable Virginia estate and gone
to war.

A bird on Bellows
A Cuckoo
A turnabout Parrot
A Grocers Shop
An Aviary
A Prussian Dragoon
A Man Smoakg
6 Small Books for
    Children
1 Fash. dres Baby...
    & other toys
6 pocket handkerchiefs

A 15,000-man force of British regulars under General William Howe landed on Long Island in August, 1776, and badly mauled the poorly trained troops under Washington's command. Throughout the summer and fall Washington lost battle after battle. By winter as they retreated through New Jersey, Washington's troops were diminishing rapidly due to death, capture, and desertion. The men were signed up only until the end of the year, and Washington was faced with the problem of somehow finding replacements. One more defeat would almost certainly crush the Revolution.

"If every nerve is not strained to recruit the New Army with all expedition," Washington wrote to a friend, "I think the game is pretty nearly up...."

But instead of polishing off Washington's band of hungry, ill-equipped rebels, the British halted their attack and set up winter quarters. General Washington decided on a desperate gamble. On Christmas night, in a storm of swirling, icy snow, his tattered army boarded a flotilla of small boats. Crossing the ice-clogged Delaware River, he routed the enemy in a devastating surprise attack. Through this brilliant strategy, Washington and his Continental Army won a decisive victory. The flame of the American Revolution burned brightly, never again to be snuffed out.

Christmas returned to Mount Vernon in 1783. After eight long years of fighting, the Revolution was finally won, and George Washington came home. His horse clattered up the roadway to the gracious mansion overlooking the Potomac just as the dusk of Christmas Eve was gathering. From all over the area came the sound of muskets being fired in salute, and the hills were set ablaze with bonfires. The General was back. Let the celebration commence.

Back up north in Massachusetts, people continued to view Christmas as "rather a day of mourning than rejoicing" well into the 1800's. One British soldier stationed in Boston prior to the start of the Revolution, noted bitterly in his diary for December 25, 1774: "Bad day; constant snow until evening, when it turned out rain and sleet. A soldier shot for desertion; the only thing done in remembrance of Christ Mass Day."

Slowly, however, the harsh Puritan influence began to abate in New England. Some of the colonists, while agreeing that the alcoholic wassail bowl might not be proper, felt that eating a

The Old World tradition of hanging mistletoe. The mistletoe kissing ball was a popular custom in Colonial America.

17

slice of mince pie or decorating their homes with a few sprigs of holly was not all that sinful. Christmas hymns were first heard in the Old North Church in Boston in 1759 and later, the Irish tradition of placing lighted candles in the windows took hold. Even though Christmas celebrations in Boston were still subdued compared to the revels in Virginia, Bishop Chase of Massachusetts in 1827 lamented, "The devil has stolen from us Christmas and converted it into a day of worldly festivity, shooting, and swearing."

There were other colonists besides those who brought their traditions, joyous or otherwise, from England. The Dutch settlers of New Amsterdam, now New York City, took great delight in keeping the spirit of Christmas. They celebrated with parties and open houses much as their distant neighbors in Virginia. Business was suspended from Saint Nicholas Eve on December 5 all the way to Twelfth Night.

And they brought with them from Holland one of our happiest Christmas traditions. On Saint Nicholas Eve, Dutch children left their wooden shoes beside the fireplace before they went to bed, just as their parents had in Holland. Every child knew that on that night Saint Nicholas, or *Sinterklaas,* as he was called in Dutch, would come riding by on a white horse and fill the shoes of good children with small presents, cakes, and candies. Bad children received only a switch. Then, as now, there were very few bad children at Christmas time.

The European ceremony of bringing in the Yule log is re-enacted at Williamsburg. The holly on top was used to kindle the fire.

George Washington watches as the Yule log is brought to
Mount Vernon in this romantic painting by J. L. G. Ferris.

The Dutch *Sinterklaas* eventually turned into our own familiar
Santa Claus. Washington Irving, the noted American storyteller
who wrote marvelous yarns about Dutch colonial life, used the
cheerful character of Saint Nicholas in several of his tales. And
a divinity teacher named Clement Moore would later write the
immortal "A Visit from Saint Nicholas"—giving birth to the
rotund, red-cheeked spirit of Christmas we know today.

By 1700, thousands of German immigrants were arriving in
America from the Rhine provinces and settled, finally, in what
was then called Western Pennsylvania. It is possible that they may
have brought the delightful tradition of the Christmas tree with
them. According to other sources, however, the first Christmas
tree was set up in America by Hessian troops at Trenton just
before the fateful battle of 1776. The German colonists certainly brought along other of their Christmas customs, though,
especially the *KristKindlein,* or Christ Child, who came on
Christmas Eve, bearing presents for the children. In the 1800's,
the *KristKindlein* became Kriss Kringle, an old and bearded twin
of Santa Claus.

A typical Christmas dinner that was popular in Virginia during the 18th century. It is just as good today.

The Moravians, like the Puritans, emigrated to the American colonies to lead a simple, godly life. The first Moravian settlement, established as a mission to the Native Americans, was founded in Savannah, Georgia, in 1735. Other Moravian settlements were situated in Pennsylvania and North Carolina. While they believed in a strict interpretation of the Bible, the Moravians felt that God could be worshiped with a song in the heart and good, if simple, food on the table.

Just as in their homeland of Germany, the Moravians observed Christmas in America with a love feast which was celebrated with Scripture, music, the lighting of candles, and food. The congregation gathered in a great hall and shared a holiday meal of buns and coffee. *Lebkuchen*, Christmas cookies made with honey, almonds, and orange peel, were a traditional favorite, as was a four-sided, wooden-based cooky pyramid.

Moravians also brought the *Putz* to America—a version of the manger scene, but much more extensive. It would often include whole miniature villages and farms, backed by snow-covered hills, all lit by tiny wax candles.

Although the major observances of Christmas in Colonial times took place in the settlements along the Eastern seaboard, there was one recorded celebration far away on the shores of Lake Huron, now St. Ignace, Michigan. The Native Americans of that isolated outpost honored the birthday of the Christ Child with an Epiphany (Twelfth Day) pageant. Father Jean Enjalran, a French Jesuit missionary, described the proceedings.

On January 6, 1679, he wrote, "All the [Native Americans], but especially the Hurons, professed a special devotion for the all-endearing mystery of our Lord Jesus Christ. They themselves entreated the priest, long before the feast day, to celebrate it in a most solemn manner." He reported that the children constructed a grotto for the Nativity scene, after which the Native Americans went to confession and attended midnight Mass.

The Hurons, having been told of the long-ago pilgrimage of the Magi to Bethlehem, wanted to re-enact the happening. They chose three chiefs to bring gifts of polished shells to the infant Jesus. Then a procession, led by a man carrying a star attached to a pole, marched into the church, and the ancient ritual was acted out. Afterwards the priest carried the statue of Jesus around the village. Finally, the Hurons invited their neighbors, the Al-

The Moravians observed a "feast of love" with a simple meal of buns and coffee just as they had done in Germany.

gonquins, to join them in a feast "at which they exhorted each other to obey Jesus Christ, who was the true Master of the World."

A traveler going back in time to the Colonial era in America would assuredly find some familiar customs, but the visitor would discover many more missing. Today, the Christmas tree enjoys a central role in the Yuletide pageantry. Although a few trees were festooned with baubles in early America, the idea of a decorated tree did not really become popular until the late 1800's. Except for the lucky Dutch children of New Amsterdam, there were few presents exchanged. And even though Christmas was celebrated by most of the inhabitants of the new land, it was not an official holiday. At Monticello, Thomas Jefferson would make a brief religious note of the day and then go to work in his study.

But the colorful parade of nationalities that today makes up our nation had already begun. Christmas customs from the Old World were rapidly being incorporated into those of the New. And then as now, the spirit was unmistakable: thanks for the past, joy for the present, and hope for the future.

A Christmas Collection of Toys

Christmas did not become a time for giving children a large number of presents until the late 1800's. A single toy was all that was hoped for by most children in the Colonial period, although as always, some parents were more indulgent than others.

17th-century doll

18th-century English "peddler doll"

Wind-up merry go-round

Mechanical toy kitchen

Girl feeding a parrot

Rooster pull toy

25

Early 19th-century versions of the Jack in the Box

18th-century doll with a basket

Wooden schoolhouse

Wooden Noah's Ark with all the animals

Metal toy coach

Wooden boy-doll from the 1800's

Carrying Christmas Throughout the Land

Thomas Jefferson took office in 1801 and immediately cast his eyes westward to the great, untamed continent that lay beyond the Mississippi River. He commissioned Meriwether Lewis and William Clark to undertake what turned out to be one of the most important expeditions in American history—the exploration of the northern territory in hopes of finding an overland route to the Pacific.

On December 25th, 1804, Lewis and Clark were 1,600 miles up the Missouri River in their winter camp near what is now Stanton, North Dakota. On that day, Clark wrote in his diary:

"I was awakened before Day by a discharge of 3 platoons from the Party and the french [boatmen], the men merrily Disposed, I gave them all a little Taffia [rum] and permitted 3 cannon fired, at raising Our flag. Some Men Went out to hunt & the others to Dancing and Continued until 9 o'clock P.M. when the frolic ended &c."

Like thousands of other Americans who found themselves in strange and distant places, Lewis and Clark carried Christmas with them and celebrated it wherever they were with whatever they could find at hand.

Many of the early explorers of the American continent have left behind accounts of Christmas along the trail. The celebrations were not always very grand. Captain John Fremont, known as the Pathfinder, used one Christmas Day to brush up on his law study with a set of borrowed books. One member of Fremont's expedition to California in 1845 noted in his diary that for Christmas dinner they had a small change in the usual menu. Instead of eating a horse, they ate one of their own worn-out pack mules.

But if Christmas was simple, it could sometimes be spectacular. In 1853, the government sent out a party led by Army Lieutenant Amiel Whipple to explore possible routes for a transcontinental railroad. The exhausted surveyors spent Christmas in an open camp in nothern Arizona shivering through subzero temperatures. Even so, as Lt. Whipple noted, the Christmas spirit burned brightly: "The fireworks were decidedly magnificent. Tall, isolated pines surrounding the camp were set on fire. The flames leaped to the treetops, and then, dying away, sent up innumerable brilliant sparks."

Soldiers, who are often the loneliest people in the world on Christmas Day, seem to have a special talent for keeping Christmas even under the worst of circumstances. In 1861, Confederate General Robert E. Lee, stationed in Coosawatchie, South Carolina, far from his home in Virginia, despaired of getting a proper Christmas present for his daughter. On Christmas morning he plucked a small bouquet of flowers and mailed them to her with the note:

"I send you some sweet violets that I gathered for you this morning . . .whose crystals glittered in the bright sun like

Lewis and Clark seek guidance from a Native American on the trail during their historic two-year exploration to find a route to the Pacific Ocean.

Preparing for Christmas: A Currier and Ives lithograph
(*above*) and a painting by Winslow Homer (*below*).

diamonds, and formed a brooch of rare beauty and sweetness which could not be fabricated by the expenditure of a world of money...Occupy yourself in aiding those more helpless than yourself. Think always of your father."

As America grew during the 1800's, it literally became a land of a hundred different Christmases. In each part of the country, the accent, the style, and sometimes even the language of the Christmas observance were different, but the message of charity and good cheer was the same.

Frontiersmen and pioneers alike led lonely lives, and Christmas meant an opportunity to get together with others, to call a halt to their back-breaking labor, and, in many cases, to let off steam in rowdy carousing. One widespread custom was the pre-Christmas turkey shoot. Not only did it provide food for the holiday table, it allowed for some satisfyingly loud noises, and brisk competition in marksmanship, too.

The Quakers along the Eastern seaboard kept a very quiet Christmas. They termed it simply "the Day called Christmas," and for many years took no official notice of the day at all. They opened their shops and worked in their factories as always. Like the Puritans, they took the word of the Bible literally and, as Christmas is not mentioned there, they ignored it. In 1812, when the Pennsylvania State Legislature adjourned for a two-week holiday, a Quaker newspaper chastised the legislators for wasting the taxpayers' money to "draw three dollars a day for eating Christmas pies."

Pennsylvania had several interesting Christmas customs in those days. One that the children must have particularly enjoyed was called "barring out the schoolmaster." A day or two before Christmas, the children would lock their teacher outside the schoolhouse, allowing him to get back in only if he promised to give each pupil a small Christmas gift.

"Belsnickling" was the unwieldy name for another Pennsylvania custom. The German Belsnickel was one of the Old World mythical spirits of Christmas who visited houses just before Christmas and gave the children toys — or switches — depending on their behavior in the past year.

The famous Mummers' Parade in Philadelphia held each year on New Year's Day originated with the English settlers of the Delaware River Valley. In the 1700's and 1800's, costumed and masked groups would go from house to house on Christmas Eve presenting little plays in return for money, or cakes, cider, and beer.

Christmas with a French flavor was celebrated in rather widely separated areas. In New Orleans, the flower-scented, mild air of the holiday season sparkled with the customs of Old France. Christmas lasted a whole week for the fun-loving Creoles of a century ago. Families gathered together, many coming from distant plantations or small settlements in other parts of Louisiana, all meeting in New Orleans.

After a solemn midnight Mass at St. Louis Cathedral, *réveillon* began. Symbolizing the wanderings of the Three Wise Men, *réveillon* was the traditional Christmas morning feast. It would usually include *daube glacé* (a jellied meat dish), a rich rum cake, and *Café Brûlot*. Grownups would then stay up and talk most of the night, but the children, having hung their stockings, went to bed to await *Papa Noël*'s arrival.

Papa Noël, the French Santa Claus, filled the stockings with candies and small toys. The real explosion of gift-giving would not take place until *Le Jour de l'An,* New Year's Day. There would most likely be a crèche, too, a replica of the manger scene in Bethlehem, for children and adults alike to enjoy.

Far to the north, other French-born settlers were celebrating Noël in somewhat similar ways. The fur trappers around the Great Lakes also kept the tradition of *réveillon.* Their menu varied from the elegant one in New Orleans, however. Roast pig, goose, beef, chicken pie, and a pastry filled with chopped beef called "bear paws" would be followed by sausage, head-cheese, fruits, nuts, and cake.

The Christmas customs of the Old World often took on new meanings when they came to America. The Norsemen burned a huge oak log once a year to honor Thor, the god of thunder. In England it was considered good luck to keep an unburned part of the Yule log all year. To the slaves in the Missouri Territory, however, the Yule log had a special significance. As long as the Yule log burned on the hearth of the big house, they were let off from work. Naturally, they took time to carefully choose the biggest and greenest log fresh from the woods, and it was not unknown for them to sprinkle the burning log with water to prolong the burning time.

Christmas is where you find it. A fairly well supplied party on the frontier *(above)*, and a loving couple separated by the Civil War *(below)* celebrate Christmas as best they can.

A cheerful Christmas cup helps to smooth a rough winter passage for these sailors.

In Leadville and Denver, where mine owners had become millionaires overnight, the holiday parties were often sumptuous dinner dances where men and women dressed in evening clothes danced until dawn. Christmas trees were set up in the great houses. Along with decorations, the trees were loaded with costly gifts for all the guests.

"They think nothing of giving Christmas and New Year's presents worth from $100 to $200," said one visitor. "A nice diamond ring, pin, or a gold watch and chain" were common.

Up in the stark, miserable gold or silver camps, the lonely miners held their own sparse but joyous Christmas. They would fire their pistols into the air and bang their tin dinner plates together to make a happy Yuletide sound and then sit down to a meager dinner. One old-timer recalled a Christmas spent with two friends: "I took out of my belt two heavy (gold) nuggets and gave one to each of them. It was a poor enough gift. Gold was a common commodity with us. They'd have appreciated a hot biscuit more."

In the cattle country of Texas, cowboys celebrated Christmas pretty much the way they celebrated everything else, with a dance. As one historian of the Old West pointed out, "A round-up's close, Christmas, New Year's Eve or some purely personal achievement of local interest, all were valid excuses for going to town to visit the dance hall."

The problem was that until the late 1800's there weren't very many women to dance with. Many a rancher would gladly ride 200 miles just to dance with a lady. For those who couldn't or wouldn't make such a long trip, the cowhands staged what were called "heifer brand" dances. A few of the cowboys would tie bandanas around their arms and take the lady's part in the dance. They may not have been very graceful, but the cowpokes seemed to enjoy the fun anyway.

One part of the West where there were more women was Salt Lake City, the home of the much-married Mormons. But in the first years of its settlement, the late 1840's, there was little time for any kind of dancing. Most pioneers who went west were looking for good, green farmland. The Mormons, however, had purposely sought out the uninviting territory near the Great Salt Lake to escape the religious persecution they had suffered in previous settlements.

The first two Christmases there were bleak ones, as the Mormons could not afford to take time off from clearing their lands to celebrate. It was not until 1849 that 150 Mormons gathered for a Christmas dinner at the home of Brigham Young, the second president of the Mormon Church, who had led his people to their new settlement. As the colony became more prosperous, Christmas parties at Young's home became a tradition. Children were given toys or more useful presents like woolen scarves and mittens. Religious services were simple and the day started with a prayer meeting at seven, followed by an exchange of gifts.

Out on the great prairies of Nebraska, Kansas, and Iowa, Christmas was often a community affair, where the farming families from miles around would gather in whatever public building was available. The Christmas Eve observance held by three denominations in Iowa's Franklin County Court House in 1868 was typical. They had hoped to have a large evergreen tree for the children, but evergreens were hard to come by on the prairie. Then someone remembered a stand of tall cedars along the Iowa River, about twenty miles away. The Reverend L. N. Call and a deacon volunteered to make the trip through freezing weather to bring one back. The decorated tree, plus presents for everyone, made the day a decided success.

Minnesota had farmers, too, but was mainly populated by fur traders, miners, and lumbermen. Its Scandinavian settlers kept

New Yorkers enjoy a winter day in a Currier and Ives lithograph,
Central Park in Winter.

their own colorful Old World customs, including the charming
one of setting out sheaves of wheat on Christmas Eve for
the birds.

The Spanish influence in frontier America was far-flung, its
roots dating back many centuries. All the way from Santa Fe,
throughout the southwest and up into California, the Spanish-
Americans practiced the customs of the past. *Los Pastores* (The
Shepherds), an old miracle play, was acted out in many parts of
the southwest. It was usually presented out-of-doors, and often
lasted as long as five hours. The basic theme was the age-old
struggle between the forces of Good and Evil, shown as taking
place in the Holy Land. The shepherds on their way to Bethlehem
were stopped and harassed by the Devil, but all came out well
in the end.

Las Posadas (The Lodgings) is one segment of *Los Pastores,* and
was given far more often. A procession, with many people play-
ing various roles, acted out Joseph and Mary's journey to
Bethlehem and their desperate search for an inn. Beginning nine
days before Christmas, the procession went to a different house
each night. The owner at first refused admittance, but eventually

let everyone in. They prayed before the manger, or *nacimiento*, and then dancing and feasting began.

Children were most fond of the *piñata*, always a big part of the festivities. It was a fragile earthen jar decorated to look like an animal or almost anything else, and filled with candies and small gifts. It was suspended from the ceiling and the blind-folded children were handed sticks to try and break the *piñata*, whereupon the candies tumbled out and the children tumbled onto them.

And what about those original inhabitants—the Native Americans? They already had their own gods, their own celebrations. But they watched with interest as missionaries, settlers, soldiers, and trappers all kept Christmas in the European tradition. Eventually, the pagan and Christian observances began to blend, sometimes evolving into fascinating new ones.

Some of the native peoples, noting that the newly come Americans seemed to celebrate Christmas with more than ample feasting, called it the Big Eating. Another term for it was Kissing Day—so named from the habit of French trappers of kissing one another when exchanging gifts. The Christmas tree was adopted with great joy by Native American tribes who already worshiped the evergreeen as the "ever-living" tree.

Eskimos, in the frozen lands of the north, observed their own festival of midwinter, *Sinck tuck*, with costumed folk dancing, feasting, and gift-giving. Each year one village would entertain another, and the next year exchange the honor. White explorers brought the Christian Christmas to the people of the north. Some areas were settled by Russians who carried their Eastern Orthodox religion to the new communities. In Sitka, the old English custom of "Christmas waits" was practiced by men who carried a star on a long pole and wandered through the town singing carols. Others went visiting, dressed in costumes and masks, remaining silent while their hosts tried to guess who they were.

Colorful or somber, rowdy or religious, lavish or meager, the Christmas celebrations of pioneer America all merged to form a potpourri of optimistic faith in a new country. Christmas was being kept, and slowly the traditions of many people began to blend into a national heritage with a unique character all its own.

Early American Christmas Decorations

The early Americans made home Christmas decoration into an art. Using fresh greenery, fruits, flowers, or just about anything that was handy, they transformed their houses into brilliant Christmas settings. The illustrations on these pages reflect the ingenuity and imagination of our ancestors in adorning their homes at holiday time.

Even such simple items as bread loaves could be used to create a Christmas decoration.

A variety of decorations from
Colonial Williamsburg: Swags of
magnolia decorated with lemons,
limes, and pine cones adorn a
double door *(right);* an elegant
sitting room *(below right);* and
a pewter bowl of greens, holly
berries, and pine cones *(below).*

A decorated Williamsburg house *(above)*
and a spectacular wreath *(right)* made
of magnolia leaves, fruits, and boxwood.

Three views of a 19th-century Christmas: A richly decorated dining room *(left);* a reconstructed Michigan house from 1830 adorned with holiday greens *(right);* and a Christmas tree chock-full of ornaments *(above).*

The popularity of the minuet had passed and George
Washington's guests at a Christmas party at Mount Vernon
in 1789 start up a lively Virginia Reel in this painting
by J. L. G. Ferris. The General, who was not a bad
dancer in his day, had apparently decided to sit this
one out and leave it to the youngsters.

Christmas with the First Family

The famous structure on Pennsylvania Avenue, which has housed every President since John Adams, was not a very impressive-looking building when it was first occupied in 1800. Set not far from a dismal swamp, it was cold, damp, and drafty. Just to stay comfortable in its unfinished rooms, the Adams family had to keep thirteen fireplaces constantly roaring. Nevertheless, Christmas is always a time to do the best with what you have, and it was the stern John Adams who threw the first children's Christmas party at the White House, in honor of his granddaughter, Susanna.

It was a great success, undoubtedly helped along by the irrepressible spirits of the First Lady, Abigail Adams. The grand ballroom was hung with greenery, cakes and punch were served, and a small orchestra played gay tunes. Caroling and lively games made up the entertainment.

One small guest, carried away by the excitement, broke one of Susanna's brand new doll's dishes. Four-year-old Susanna had not been born into one of America's most powerful families for nothing, and immediately retaliated by biting off the nose of her friend's doll. President Adams had to step in to restore order.

43

The next inhabitant of the White House, Thomas Jefferson, was a widower. Christmas would have been a lonely time for him had it not been for his beloved grandchildren. In 1805, six of them came to spend the holiday with him. Dolley Madison, wife of the then Secretary of State, acting as the President's official hostess, invited more than 100 of his grandchildren's friends to a whopper of a Christmas party. Jefferson enjoyed himself so hugely that he even brought out his violin and played while the children danced. Most Christmas parties at the Jefferson White House, however, were elegant affairs where guests dined on local American foods prepared in the European fashion by his French chef and accented with all kinds of exotic delicacies.

Andrew Jackson

Andrew Jackson, our seventh President, was known as a tough-skinned campaigner and the hero of the War of 1812. Yet there was another, softer side to "Old Hickory." His wife Rachel had died soon after his election to the Presidency and his niece, Emily Donelson, was acting as hostess at the White House. One Christmas week, six children were visiting, four of Mrs. Donelson's and two of the President's grandchildren.

They all pestered the servants and any other grownup who would listen to find out if there really was a Santa Claus. Not entirely satisfied with the answers they were getting, six-year-old Johnny Donelson decided to go straight to the President himself. Johnny asked him point-blank if Santa would come to their house that night. The President told the boy he would have to wait and see.

The children, while hanging their own stockings on Christmas Eve, insisted that President Jackson hang one, too. The next morning, the crusty old general wept as he pulled small gifts, including a corncob pipe, from his stocking, filled secretly in the night by the family. Young Johnny, surrounded by his own pile of presents, had his answer. Santa had come after all.

The little boy had another question for his granduncle. Did Santa Claus *always* come? The President replied that once there was a boy whose mother was dead and who had never even heard about Santa. He had no toys at all for Christmas. It was not until years later that Johnny realized that Jackson himself had been that boy.

Jackson then proceeded to call for a carriage and went out to visit an orphanage where he personally distributed the gifts he brought among the children. The next day there was a gay party at the White House replete with candies and cakes, and lots of games. The President himself joined in a snowball fight in the formal East Room—cotton balls lightly covered with starch were used as ammunition.

At last the children, covered with "snow," bid farewell and trooped across the lawn. One guest said he thought they looked like "the fairy procession in *Midsummer Night's Dream.*" Jackson shook his head. He said they made him think of the words, "Suffer the little children to come unto Me, and forbid them not, for of such is the Kingdom of God."

The first White House Christmas tree was erected by the amiable Franklin Pierce, who was elected to office in 1853. The ornamented "German Tree" was a fairly new innovation in America, but as in England, it quickly became the focus of most home Christmas celebrations. Today the national observance of the Christmas season does not officially get under way until the President lights the giant tree on the Ellipse, the park directly south of the White House.

During the bitter days of the Civil War, Christmases with the Lincolns were quiet family affairs. Characteristically, President Lincoln's last Christmas in 1864 was marked by a generous gesture of compassion. On December 24, Gideon Welles, his Secretary of the Navy, approached the President on behalf of Miss Laura Jones, of Richmond, Virginia. Three years before, she had become engaged to marry a Southerner, but had gone to Washington to nurse her ailing mother. Now that Mrs. Jones was well again, the daughter wanted desperately to go to her betrothed, but needed Presidential permission to get through the Union lines.

Mr. Welles made it clear that Miss Jones was a dedicated Southern sympathizer. The weary President said that it was all right. "The war has depopulated the country and prevented marriages enough," he commented. As an added thought, Lincoln dated his letter December 25, so Miss Jones could have it as a Christmas present.

Abraham Lincoln

Over the years, Christmas at the White House has been observed in many different ways. Our Presidents, just as all Americans, celebrate the holiday season by carrying on their own traditional regional and family customs.

Painted wood Santa Claus sculpture by John Robb

The Evolution of Santa Claus

Like almost everyone else in America, Santa Claus was an immigrant. Stories about St. Nicholas go back as far as the fourth century. In Europe, he had gone by many names—Father Christmas, *Sinterklaas, Papa Noël,* and *Kris Kringle* were just a few. In some countries he would arrive riding a white pony, in others on a camel, and one legend had him appearing on Christmas Eve sitting on the back of a wagon drawn by a team of goats. To the children of Holland, he was somewhat stern. In Germany, he was like a judge who looked at your record and handed out rewards or punishments accordingly. In America, Santa Claus was generally seen as a jollier figure. Few children believed he would come all the way from the North Pole just to bring them a switch.

The vision of Santa Claus that captured America's imagination came from an unlikely source. To amuse his children in the Christmas of 1822, Dr. Clement C. Moore, a distinguished scholar and teacher, wrote a brief verse about a man who awakens in the middle of the night and sees St. Nicholas coming down the chimney with a bundle of presents.

The poem was meant only for his family's entertainment and the learned doctor had no thought of publishing it. But it found its way into print, and eventually, the quiet scholar became one of the most beloved poets in America.

Three versions of Santa Claus. At left he arrives with half the usual reindeer. He waits patiently *(below),* and *(at bottom)* he strides in, knowing he is the most popular man at the party.

Santa Claus was always a most useful fellow. His face
is a series of envelope stickers *(above)*, and he becomes
the front and back of a 19th-century Christmas doll.

The transformation of St. Nicholas, — the tall, stern patriarch in bishop's robes of the early 1800's — into the red-suited, white-bearded, prosperous-looking, tubby and jovial Santa Claus of later years was helped along by the 1848 edition of Clement Moore's verse "A visit from St. Nicholas," illustrated by Boyd.

A long winter's nap

On, Donder and Blitzen

Down the chimney

Straight to his work

50

Santa Claus was depicted by the 19th-century American artists
in many different ways. But it was the political cartoonist,
Thomas Nast, who seemed to capture best the qualities of the
jolly gift-giver that most appealed to Americans. His series
of Santas, created in the 1860's for the *Harper's Weekly* was
an instant success.

A Victorian Christmas

In the early years of America's history, Christmas remained largely a series of local celebrations. Each community kept Christmas, or ignored the day, in its own way. Except when Christmas happened to fall on a Sunday, it was a regular working day in Boston until 1856. The Boston public schools did not close for Christmas until 1870. It took more than fifty years for Christmas to be declared a legal holiday throughout the country. In 1836, Alabama was the first state in the Union to take legal note of Christmas, and it was not until 1890 that the Oklahoma Territory followed suit.

When Christmas was observed in this land of immigrants, the celebrations were as different as the peoples themselves. Almost always these observances harked back to some dimly remembered European ritual. In North Carolina two men would get under a sheet with a steer's head sticking out and cavort around the countryside as "Old Buck," whose history can be traced back to the earliest days of Christianity.

In the Ozark Mountains, where it was possible to hear English spoken almost exactly as it was in the days of Oliver Cromwell two hundred years before, the people continued to mark Christmas Day in January according to an old European tradition, discarded long before throughout the rest of the world.

In Georgia, a Major Jones once tried to recapture the Scandinavian tradition of leaving presents on the doorsteps of friends on Christmas Eve. Major Jones wanted to make a present of himself to his girl friend. He crawled inside a meal

An ardent Victorian tests the charms of mistletoe.

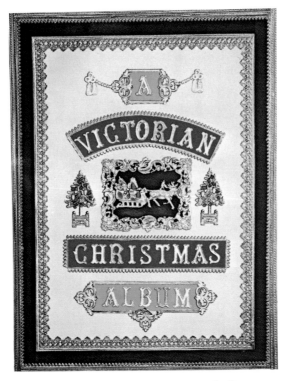

Four collages by Leslie Dorsey, made from materials of
the time, capture the spirit of a Victorian Christmas.

sack and had himself suspended from a hook in front of her
door. It is not certain whether he won the lady in question or
not. But hopefully the story had a happy ending, for the ardent
major spent a most unpleasant Christmas Eve. A dog barked at
him all through the freezing night, and he got a little "seasick"
as he swayed to and fro in the gusty wind.

By 1876, as the United States was celebrating its centennial
birthday, the broad outlines of what we now call a "traditional"
American Christmas were formed. The early Colonial settlers
might have found the celebration somewhat puzzling. But we
would feel right at home. Almost all the customs we follow now
were just as common then.

The following description is typical of the way Christmas
might have been celebrated by a family in New York City in 1876:

The Christmas season started early. The holiday shopping
alone took a long time. Most people were members of large
families, and there were a great many gifts to get. The city was
filled with specialty shops where one could go just to buy
English linen or French lace. In addition, the first of the large
city department stores had appeared with their huge selection
of goods. As always, shopping for the children was the most fun.

German mechanical toys appeared in great variety on the shelves. These clockwork devices, complete with moving parts, were particularly prized by boys and girls alike. One of the more popular models was a chicken which popped up and clucked happily over a pair of painted tin eggs, and another had a pair of boxers in a small ring who flailed away at each other ferociously.

Christmas in New York was a social season as well as a spiritual one in 1876, and among the most popular holiday entertainments were the Christmas ice-skating parties, which had become seasonal events ever since the Central Park ponds were opened in the 1860's. These parties were popular not only as family outings, but also because they afforded young men and women an opportunity for courting—under the watchful eyes of their parents. As one publication of the day pointed out, "the privilege a gentleman enjoys of imparting instruction in the art to his fair companion is to enjoy a combination of duty and pleasure not often within reach, and no relation is more calculated to produce tender attachments than that of pupil and tutor under such circumstances."

Decorating the home at Christmas time was a custom that went back to the days of ancient Rome, but it was raised to a new art in the late 1800's. In the weeks before Christmas, houses were festooned with bright seasonal greenery, flowers, and decorations. One of the most favored flowers was the poinsettia, originally imported from Mexico, whose brilliant red leafy bracts represent the flaming star of Bethlehem.

By 1876, the centerpiece of any proper Christmas was a large, ornamented evergreen tree set up inside the home. This dazzling idea was originally a German innovation which made its first appearance in America during the early 19th century. After England's Queen Victoria and her German husband, Prince Albert, set up a tree in Windsor Castle in 1841, the custom spread rapidly throughout the entire western world.

Decorating the tree and filling its boughs with presents was a very serious business, as one contemporary account of a New York doctor and his family shows:

"Marian drew long strings of bright red holly berries threaded like beads upon fine cord, and festooned them in graceful garlands from the boughs which the Doctor had arranged with tiny candles. Long pieces of fine wire were passed through the candles at the bottom. These were clasped over the stem of each

Christmas shopping at a toy store on Broadway and Canal streets in New York City in 1865.

56

In this 1834 lithograph, a family walks home through
the park after a long round of the department stores.

branch and twisted underneath, taking care to have a clear space
above each wick so nothing might catch fire. Strings of bright
berries, small bouquets of paper flowers, strings of beads, tiny
flags of gay ribbons, stars and shields of bright paper, lace bags
filled with colored candies, knots of bright ribbons, all home-
made, made a brilliant show. At last the more important presents
were brought down from an upper room. Dolls for each of the
little girls were seated on the boughs. A large cart for Eddie, with
two horses prancing before it, drove gayly among the top
branches. Beneath the branches Marian placed a set of wooden

animals for Eddie, while from the topmost branch was suspended a gilded cage, ready for the canary bird purchased for the pet-loving Lizzie."

Christmas Eve was probably the busiest night of the year in most American homes. There was the last-minute wrapping of packages to be done, and rushing a belated Christmas card across town to that old friend who had somehow been forgotten until his card arrived late in the afternoon. Many of the house decorations, too, waited until the eleventh hour because there was an old belief that some Christmas greenery would bring misfortune to the family if brought into the house before Christmas Eve.

The night before Christmas was also a time for strolling bands, carolers, and handbell ringers who would come by to serenade each home with a rendition of such carols as "O, Come, All Ye Faithful" or "It Came Upon a Midnight Clear." Each group would be invited inside for a glass of punch and perhaps given a few coins.

A brightly decorated tree was the center-piece of every proper Victorian Christmas.

Harper's Weekly, a leading publication of the 19th century, offered their readers this Christmas drawing in 1866.

In a great many homes, it became a Christmas Eve tradition to gather the family together for a reading of the Charles Dickens classic story, *A Christmas Carol.* No writer ever loved Christmas more than Dickens, and his tale of the redemption of Ebenezer Scrooge was felt, on both sides of the Atlantic, to be a perfect reflection of the spirit of the Victorian Christmas.

At long last, the young children were sent to bed after hanging their stockings for Santa Claus to fill later that night. Like the Christmas celebration itself, Santa Claus had not always been popular in all parts of America. Many concerned clergymen preached against Santa Claus from their pulpits because they feared that the emergence of such a folk culture here would draw people's attention away from their celebration of the miracle of Christ's birth. But the idea of a jolly gift-giver from the North Pole proved to be so popular that he became a permanent part of every American Christmas celebration.

Christmas Day got started early as the children went through their stocking presents, and eventually made such a din that the parents had to get up and go downstairs to open the presents

Christmas tree in the home of Orville and Wilbur Wright in Ohio,
as it might have looked in the early 1870's.

under the tree. After breakfast, there might be a mid-morning church service and then the family would walk back home for Christmas dinner.

There was an old English saying that "the Devil himself dare not appear during Christmas for fear of being baked in a pie." American ovens were kept just as busy. A typical Christmas dinner would include a roast turkey with cranberry sauce, a boiled ham, goose pie, coleslaw, squash, beets, lemon custard, and a cranberry pie. In the more elegant homes they might add turtle soup, oyster pie, and a flaming plum pudding.

The plum pudding would come last, its eerie blue flames casting strange shadows throughout the room. The pudding was dotted inside with small silver coins that could be kept by whoever bit into one.

While the adults were still talking at the dinner table over nuts and wine, the children would steal away into another room to get ready to put on their own Christmas play for the family and guests. Once they were in costume and their props were all in place, the rest of the household would be signaled to come to the parlor where they would watch the children put on a dramatic reading of "'Twas the Night Before Christmas" complete with the sound of offstage sleigh bells and reindeer hooves.

After the play the parlor would ring with the sounds of children's games as the whole family joined in "Blind Man's Buff" and "Hunt-the-Slipper." Later that night there would be one more Christmas cake—this one coated with marzipan and sugar. Finally, as it grew dark outside, the candles would be lit on the tree and the family would gather around it and tell stories. Ghost stories were the most favored and the scarier the better.

When we think about a traditional, "old-fashioned" American Christmas, this is the kind most of us turn to. And rightly so, for those Victorian worthies knew how to keep Christmas and they established a holiday tradition that is as fresh today as it was a hundred years ago.

Christmas cards quickly became as much a part of the season as Santa Claus and the last-minute shopping rush.

Season's Greetings

By 1876, the sending of Christmas cards, which is now so much a part of our holiday tradition, was just gaining popularity. The first known card was created in England, in 1843, by the artist John Calcott Horsley for a wealthy client to send to his friends. It showed a happy family sitting at their Christmas table and had the inscription, "Merry Christmas and a Happy New Year to You" below the drawing.

Louis Prang, who came to America in 1850 from Breslau, Germany, is considered "the father of the American Christmas card." A superb craftsman, he developed a prosperous lithography business in Boston, and in 1874 he began producing Christmas cards. His early American cards, delicately crafted, are masterpieces of 19th-century lithography, and were prized at the time as works of art. Christmas cards have been gaining in popularity ever since.

The early cards created by Louis Prang
(above) were simple. But as the use
of cards increased, they turned
more ornate and irregularly shaped cards
like the one *(at top)* crafted by
John A. Lowell became popular.

A Christmas Sampler

The Christmas holiday season in early America was both a time for relaxation and a period of furious activity. America was primarily a rural and agricultural nation in the 1700's and there were few people who could afford to take a summer vacation. Summer was the time for growing food and undertaking the construction projects that were so essential to the survival of a young nation. By the time winter set in, the crops had been harvested and the storing of provisions accomplished. But instead of settling down for a long winter's rest, many Americans found themselves caught up in the bustle of Christmas preparations. There were hunts to organize, parties to give, houses to decorate and, of course, holiday dinners to prepare.

In the pages that follow you will find several Yuletide decoration projects adapted for use today from the techniques of those early days. Some traditional Colonial holiday recipes, brought up to date, are included as well. To add to your enjoyment of keeping a traditional Christmas, you will also find a selection of Christmas carols composed by Americans.

Corn husk dolls

The early settlers in the American colonies found that the corn stalk not only provided them with a new food, but also a source of pleasure for children who had to create their own playthings. Making a corn husk doll like the one in your Christmas package is not as difficult as it may look. Essentially, it is just a simple cross decorated into the shape of a doll. Once you learn the basic form, you can shape these dolls into any position you like. They may be used on the tree as ornaments or given as presents.

To make one you will need about 8 corn husks, 3 feet of florist's wire, an ounce of glycerin and one soft rubber or styrofoam ball about ¾ of an inch in diameter.

Spread the glycerin on the corn husks and soak in hot water about 15 minutes until flexible.

To make the arms, cut off a 3-inch length of wire, and cut one of the husks into a 1- by 4-inch rectangle. Lay the wire lengthwise in the middle of the husk and roll it up as tightly as you can, fixing both ends with florist's wire (Fig. 1).

Cut a second husk into the same size as the first, 1 by 4 inches. Make a 2-inch-long mark in the middle of a third husk. Wrap the third husk around the first one and wind securely with wire along the length of your mark. Now take the ends of the second husk, fold them back to the middle and secure them with wire (Fig. 2). Put aside.

To make the body, take a 4-inch piece of wire and stick it about halfway into the ball. This will form a base for the head. Attach the arms about an inch below the head, and tie by wrapping wire around the neck and body several times. Make sure this basic form is secure and the rest will be easy.

Cut a 2- by 6-inch piece of husk and wire it around the head (Fig. 3). Bring the rest of the husk down and secure it to the wire about ½ inch below

Fig. 1

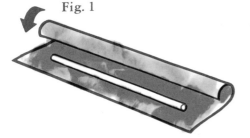

Fig. 2

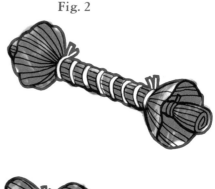

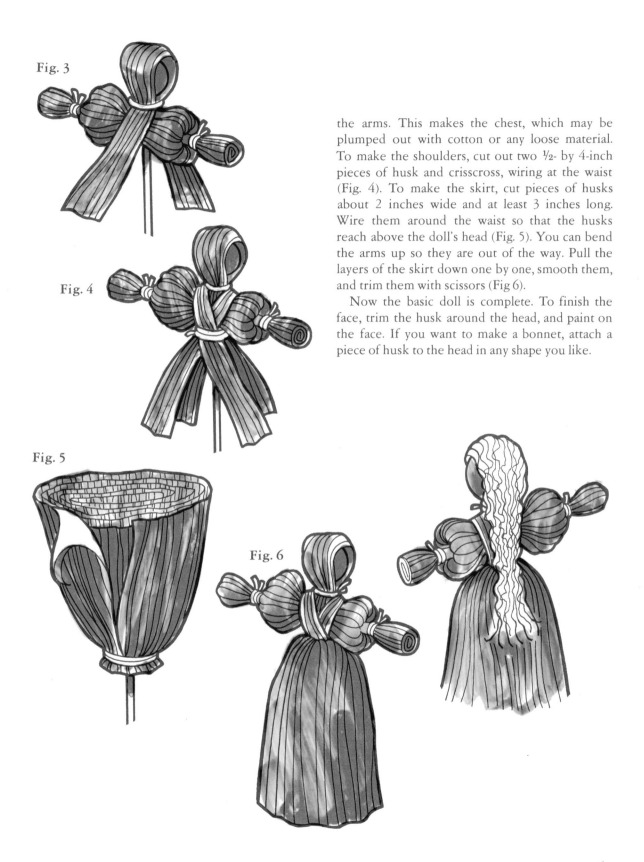

Fig. 3

Fig. 4

Fig. 5

Fig. 6

the arms. This makes the chest, which may be plumped out with cotton or any loose material. To make the shoulders, cut out two ½- by 4-inch pieces of husk and crisscross, wiring at the waist (Fig. 4). To make the skirt, cut pieces of husks about 2 inches wide and at least 3 inches long. Wire them around the waist so that the husks reach above the doll's head (Fig. 5). You can bend the arms up so they are out of the way. Pull the layers of the skirt down one by one, smooth them, and trim them with scissors (Fig 6).

Now the basic doll is complete. To finish the face, trim the husk around the head, and paint on the face. If you want to make a bonnet, attach a piece of husk to the head in any shape you like.

Patchwork project

It is an old Colonial tradition to use bits of material from the family sewing box to create something new. Here are two projects which are simple to make and will provide bright Christmas time decorations for around the house.

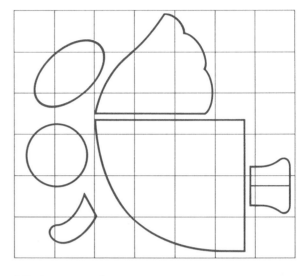

Quilted Christmas stocking

Take any two pieces of brightly colored material and cut out a pair of identically sized stocking shapes. Stitch around all the sides but leave the top open. Turn inside out. Stuff the stocking with Dacron fiberfill, cotton or other loose cloth, cut to the shape of your stocking. Sew the top together by hand. With a darning needle pull yarn through, making a square pattern, and knot tightly on each side of the stocking. Once you have made the basic stocking shape you can decorate it with bells, tassels, decals, or anything you like. Remember though, this stocking is for decoration only. You won't get any presents in it.

Flying angel

Copy the patterns for the angel onto a large piece of paper with a 4″ grid. Cut out the patterns for the wings and the body and two for the halo, and pin them to a red material, and those for the head, feet, and arms (two for each), to a white material. When cutting the material around the patterns, allow ½ inch for seams. If you are going to put a dress on the angel, do it now. Then sew the body and wings together, cut a single piece of white backing to fit and sew together, leaving openings for the arms and feet. Stuff the body, the arms, and the feet. Attach arms and feet to the body. Draw the face on one of the white circles for the head, stuff, and sew. Add a head of curls, using yarn and a darning needle. Sew and stuff the halo and attach it to the head. Then sew the head to the body.

Pomander balls and sachets

These old-fashioned creations make delightful Christmas tree ornaments that are thoughtful presents as well. Once they have been used to decorate the tree or the table they may be hung in your closet or placed in a bureau drawer. The scent of a pomander ball can last for years.

Pomander balls

A thin-skinned orange is the usual start of a pomander ball, but almost any fruit can be used. A lemon makes a very attractive tree ornament.

Take an orange and stud it over its entire surface with whole cloves. You might need a skewer or heavy needle to make holes to get the cloves into the orange without breaking them. For decoration, the cloves can be loosely spaced, but the pomander ball will work better as a closet hanging if the surface is entirely covered with cloves. Once the fruit is studded, put it in a bowl containing a mixture of cinnamon, allspice, and orrisroot. Leave the fruit in the bowl for at least five days and roll it around in the mixture twice a day.

When the fruit has dried out, put it in a piece of netting and tie it with a bow of velvet ribbon or satin.

Sachets

A sachet is any small bag containing scented herbs or perfumed powders. You can experiment with these combinations as much as you like. This fragrant wood sachet is typical. Take ½ pound of sandalwood powder and ½ teaspoon of cedarwood oil and mix them together in a jar.* Seal the jar tightly and let it stand for a week. Make sachet bags by folding 4" x 8" pieces of cloth in half and sewing up each side as far as 1 inch from the top of the bag, about ½ inch in from the sides. Turn the sacks inside out. Any material may be used, but it should be tightly enough woven to hold the mixture. Fill the bags, gather the unsewn ends, and tie tightly with ribbon.

Christmas Dinner

Christmas dinner in America has, since the earliest Colonial days, reflected the native tastes and traditions of our forefathers and, also, included many of the unfamiliar foods they found available in the New World.

While the stern New Englanders for many years kept Christmas in the simplest manner possible, when they celebrated it at all, the Virginia cavaliers engaged in a week-long series of banquets and buffets. The plum puddings and mince pies of their English mother country were an important part of the ceremonies, and one of the highlights of a Virginia Christmas would be an invitation to Mount Vernon where guests were treated to a sumptuous meal and several rounds of George Washington's incendiary eggnog.

In Baltimore, widely different ethnic backgrounds mingled during the Colonial period, producing an Anglo-German tradition of serving a roast bird with sauerkraut. Early Dutch settlers in New York celebrated with masses of hearty food, especially on New Year's Day when they held open house. Tables laden with baked hams, turkey, game birds, and lobster salad were set up, and doors were thrown open to any friend who wished to come in and toast the new year.

For a while it was a common practice for New Yorkers to advertise in the local newspapers the times they would be receiving guests. They had to stop that, however, when startled hostesses found themselves entertaining total strangers who had read the papers and came by for a free meal.

In New Orleans, the Christmas season had the Creole touch. The citizens of New Orleans, like the Dutch, saved their biggest celebrations for New Year's Day. A Louisiana New Year's dinner generally began with oysters and consommé, followed by fillet of sole stuffed with crab. Then the main course of roast turkey and yams, mashed potatoes, cauliflower, and salad was served, topped off with vanilla ice cream, flaming bananas, and that New Orleans specialty, *Café Brûlot.*

The New World provided an interesting collection of comestibles for the pioneers' Christmas table. Turkey and other native birds, and wild game—including squirrel, venison, buffalo, elk, antelope, prairie dog, and grizzly bear—often became part of the newly come settlers' holiday fare. The Indians introduced cranberries and squash.

As the nation expanded westward, more combinations of the old and new took root, eventually developing into unique regional holiday menus, all, however, carrying on the American tradition of lavish Christmas hospitality.

The recipes in this section are all adapted from the traditional ones of the period and modernized for present-day cooking techniques.

George Washington's eggnog

This potent holiday drink was a favorite of the general's. It is made in Virginia to this day, in exactly the same proportions. This recipe makes about three quarts.

   1 pint brandy
  ½ pint rye whiskey
  4 ounces sherry
  4 ounces rum
12 eggs, separated
 ¾ cup sugar
  1 quart milk
  1 quart cream

Combine liquor. Beat egg yolks in a large bowl until thick, then beat in sugar. Gradually add liquor, then milk and cream while continuing to beat. Beat egg whites to stiff, not dry, peaks; fold into liquid mixture. Cover and refrigerate for at least 5 days before serving.

Sorrel soup

Anyone fortunate enough to dine with Thomas Jefferson at Monticello might start with this simple but delicious cream soup. It can be served hot or ice cold. This recipe makes 4 to 6 servings.

1 pound fresh sorrel leaves
¼ cup butter
1 medium onion, chopped
2 egg yolks, beaten
1 cup light cream
3 cups chicken broth
   Salt and pepper

Wash sorrel leaves thoroughly and then dry. Chop the leaves finely. Heat butter in a skillet; add onion and cook until soft. Stir in sorrel and cook over low heat until wilted, about 5 minutes. Blend egg yolks and cream. Heat broth to boiling in a large saucepan; stir a small amount of hot broth into egg yolk-cream mixture, then stir that mixture into broth and heat thoroughly. Add sorrel mixture and salt and pepper to taste. Serve hot or refrigerate until icy cold, then serve. For a smoother soup, blend in an electric blender.

Baked stuffed fillets with creole sauce

This exotic offering was a great holiday favorite of New Orleans magnificos. Creole cooking is a spicy heritage from the original French and Spanish settlers of Louisiana. This example is quite rich, so if you prefer a simpler dish, don't stuff the fillets. Cook them according to your favorite recipe and serve with the sauce.

- ¼ cup butter
- 2 tablespoons finely chopped onion
- 2 tablespoons chopped celery
- 2 tablespoons chopped green pepper
- 2 tablespoons flour
- ½ cup milk or light cream
- ¼ teaspoon salt
- ⅛ teaspoon pepper
- ⅛ teaspoon paprika
- 2 teaspoons Worcestershire sauce
- 2 drops Tabasco
- 1 cup cooked crab meat
- 1 cup cooked coarsely chopped shrimp
- ½ teaspoon chopped parsley
- 6 flounder or sole fillets
  Melted butter
  Creole Sauce

Heat butter in a saucepan. Add onion, celery, and green pepper. Cook until ingredients are soft but not browned. Stir in flour and then milk. Cook and stir until thickened. Remove from heat; stir in seasonings, crab meat, shrimp, and parsley. Mound some stuffing on each fillet, roll up, and secure with wooden picks. Put the fillet roll-ups, leaving space between, into a greased shallow baking dish. Brush fish with melted butter. Bake at 350°F 10 to 15 minutes. Pour Creole Sauce over top. Continue baking 25 minutes.   6 servings

Creole sauce

- 4 cups canned or peeled fresh tomatoes
- 1 teaspoon salt
- ½ teaspoon thyme
- 1 bay leaf, crumbled
  Black and red pepper to taste
- 1 large clove garlic, finely chopped
- 2 tablespoons butter
- 1 tablespoon flour

Combine tomatoes, seasonings, and 1 tablespoon butter in a saucepan. Bring to a boil and cook over medium heat until sauce is reduced by half, stirring occasionally. Melt the remaining 1 tablespoon butter in a small saucepan. Blend in flour and cook over low heat until lightly browned; mix with sauce and cook 5 minutes.

Baked ham and maple syrup

This is a dish that would likely be served at one of the New Year's Day receptions in a prosperous Dutch home in New York. An old-fashioned method of preparing ham, it is extremely simple. This recipe is for a single slice of ham that serves four, but it can be expanded into a buffet dish that serves several times that many. Asparagus or broccoli were usually served with it.

- 1 ham slice (1½ inches thick)
  Cloves (optional)
- 2 teaspoons dry mustard
- 2 tablespoons cider vinegar
- ¾ cup maple syrup

Slash the fatty edge of ham several times to keep it from curling during cooking. Stud ham with cloves, if desired; put into a baking pan. Blend mustard, vinegar, and maple syrup; pour over ham. Bake at 350°F about 1 hour, basting occasionally. Remove from oven. Transfer ham to a warm platter. Set the baking pan over high heat; cook and stir to reduce liquid to a sauce consistency. Pour over ham. Serve any extra sauce separately.

Candied cranberries

2 cups fresh cranberries
1 cup sugar

Wash cranberries and spread over bottom of a shallow baking dish. Sprinkle with sugar and cover tightly. Bake at 350°F 1 hour, stirring occasionally. Chill before serving as a meat accompaniment.

New Orleans sweet potato pie

A traditional southern Christmas dish, sweet potato pie has been called "sweet potatoes for people who hate sweet potatoes." Although it looks like a dessert, it is served as a vegetable.

4 eggs
1½ cups mashed cooked sweet potatoes
⅓ cup sugar
¼ teaspoon salt
⅔ cup milk
⅓ cup orange juice
1 tablespoon honey
1 teaspoon vanilla extract
½ cup finely chopped pecans
1 unbaked 9-inch pastry shell
Whipped cream topping

Beat eggs until foamy. Mix in sweet potatoes, then sugar, salt, milk, orange juice, honey, vanilla extract, and pecans. Turn mixture into pastry shell. Bake at 450°F 10 to 15 minutes, turn oven regulator to 350°F, and continue baking about 25 minutes. Set on rack to cool. Spread whipped cream over top.

Moravian Christmas cookies

These spicy molasses cookies were a familiar treat at Moravian Christmas "Love Feasts." When they were made at times other than Christmas, they were much larger and were called cakes. This recipe makes about 10 dozen thin cookies.

¼ cup lard
¼ cup butter
1 cup molasses
½ cup firmly packed brown sugar
1 teaspoon cinnamon
1 teaspoon cloves
¾ teaspoon ginger
¾ teaspoon baking soda
3½ cups flour

Melt lard and butter together. Set aside to cool. Mix molasses and brown sugar in a bowl. Add melted fat and mix well. Blend spices, baking soda, and 1 tablespoon flour; stir into molasses mixture. Add the remaining flour. Refrigerate dough at least 4 hours. Roll out dough very thin on a floured surface. Cut into shapes and lay on greased cooky sheets. Bake at 350°F 8 to 10 minutes.

Café Brûlot

A dazzling New Orleans specialty, this after-dinner drink was once described as, "the crowning of a great dinner."

3 cups strong coffee
½ of large orange
10 cubes sugar
10 whole cloves
4 sticks cinnamon, broken in small pieces
1½ cups brandy or cognac

Prepare coffee in your favorite manner; keep hot. Turn the orange half inside out and place, flesh side up, in an earthenware bowl or chafing dish. Add sugar, cloves, and cinnamon. Pour brandy (warmed, if not using chafing dish) over the orange. Ignite the brandy, then add the hot coffee. Ladle the liquid over the orange. Serve at once in demitasse cups. This recipe will make 16 servings.

American carols

Most of our popular Christmas carols, and the custom of caroling itself, came from England. But the oldest recorded instance of caroling in America was French-inspired. In 1645, Father Barthélémy Vimont, S.J., reported that the Huron Indians at Mackinac (now Mackinaw, Michigan) met to "sing hymns in honor of the new-born Child." Another missionary of that time, Jean de Brébeuf, S.J., composed the first American carol, "Jesus is Born." It was written in the Huron language to the tune of an old French folk song.

Our best-known Christmas songs in English, however, have a much more recent origin. The verse for "It Came Upon a Midnight Clear" was written by Edmund H. Sears, a Unitarian minister of Weston, Mass., in 1849, and the rousing music was composed by Boston musician Richard S. Willis the following year. John Henry Hopkins, Jr., an Episcopalian minister, created, in 1857, both the words and the music for his classic carol "We Three Kings of Orient Are."

In 1863, the famed poet Henry Wadsworth Longfellow watched with horror as the Civil War grew, taking the lives of thousands of young men on both sides. His own son had been seriously wounded fighting for the Union. Longfellow's poem, "I Heard the Bells on Christmas Day," was a plea for a speedy end to the bloody conflict. It was set to music in 1872 by John Baptiste Calkin.

And in 1868, Phillips Brooks, later Episcopal Bishop of Massachusetts, wrote a poem for his Sunday School class inspired by the memory of a pilgrimage he had made to the Holy Land three years earlier. Set to music by Lewis Redner, it quickly became one of our favorite Christmas songs...."O Little Town of Bethlehem."

American folk music has made its own unique contribution to the roster of home-grown carols. An odd offering from the Kentucky mountains claims, "Christ was born in Bethlehem, and Mary was his niece." And one of the loveliest of American Christmas hymns, "Rise Up, Shepherd, and Follow," originated with black slaves.

Our joyful Christmas sounds also draw heavily on the heritage of the many immigrants—the Irish, the Germans, the Italians, the Poles, and the many others who brought their favorites with them across the sea.

I Heard the Bells on Christmas Day

HENRY W. LONGFELLOW   J. BAPTISTE CALKIN

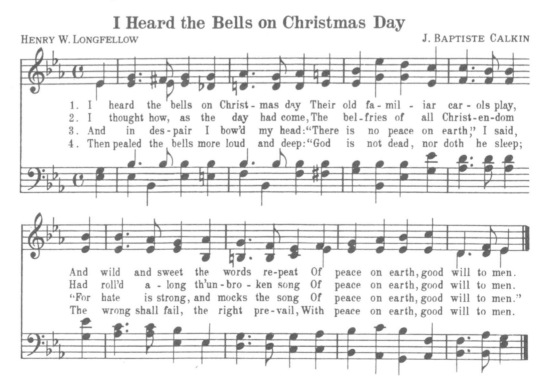

1. I heard the bells on Christ-mas day Their old fa-mil-iar car-ols play,
2. I thought how, as the day had come, The bel-fries of all Christ-en-dom
3. And in des-pair I bow'd my head:"There is no peace on earth," I said,
4. Then pealed the bells more loud and deep:"God is not dead, nor doth he sleep;

And wild and sweet the words re-peat Of peace on earth, good will to men.
Had roll'd a-long th'un-bro-ken song Of peace on earth, good will to men.
"For hate is strong, and mocks the song Of peace on earth, good will to men."
The wrong shall fail, the right pre-vail, With peace on earth, good will to men.

It Came upon the Midnight Clear

EDMUND H. SEARS

RICHARD S. WILLIS

1. It came up-on the mid-night clear, That glo-rious song of old, —
2. Still thro' the clo - ven skies they come, With peace-ful wings un - furled;
3. O ye be - neath life's crush-ing load, Whose forms are bend - ing low, —
4. For lo! the days are has-t'ning on, By proph - ets seen of old, —

From an - gels bend - ing near the earth, To touch their harps of gold: —
And still their heav'n - ly mu - sic floats O'er all the wea - ry world:
Who toil a - long the climb-ing way With pain - ful steps and slow; —
When with the ev - er - cir - cling years Shall come the time fore - told, —

"Peace on the earth, good will to men From heav'n's all gra - cious King," —
A - bove its sad and low - ly plains They bend on hov - 'ring wing, —
Look now, for glad and gold - en hours Come swift - ly on the wing; —
When the new heav'n and earth shall own The Prince of Peace their King, —

The world in sol - emn still-ness lay To hear the an - gels sing. —
And ev - er o'er its Ba - bel sounds The bless - ed an - gels sing. —
Oh rest be - side the wea - ry road And hear the an - gels sing. —
And the whole world send back the song Which now the an - gels sing. —

We Three Kings Of Orient Are

J. H. H. Jr.

John H. Hopkins Jr.

O Little Town of Bethlehem

PHILLIPS BROOKS

LEWIS H. REDNER

1. O lit - tle town of Beth - le - hem, How still we see thee lie;
2. For Christ is born of Ma - ry; And gath - ered all a - bove,
3. How si - lent - ly, how si - lent - ly, The won - drous gift is giv'n!
4. O ho - ly Child of Beth - le - hem, De - scend to us, we pray;

A - bove thy deep and dream - less sleep The si - lent stars go by:
While mor - tals sleep, the an - gels keep Their watch of won - d'ring love.
So God im - parts to hu - man hearts The bless - ings of His heav'n.
Cast out our sin, and en - ter in, Be born in us to - day.

Yet in thy dark streets shin - eth The ev - er - last - ing Light;
O morn - ing stars, to - geth - er Pro - claim the ho - ly birth;
No ear may hear His com - ing, But in this world of sin,
We hear the Christ - mas an - gels The great glad tid - ings tell;

The hopes and fears of all the years Are met in thee to - night.
And prais - es sing to God, the King, And peace to men on earth.
Where meek souls will re - ceive Him, still The dear Christ en - ters in.
O come to us, a - bide with us, Our Lord Em - man - u - el.

Index

Adams, Abigail, 43
Adams, John, 43
Adams, Susanna, 43
Alabama, 52
Albert, Prince, 56
Algonquins, 23
American Christmas carols, 65, 74-77
American Revolution, 10, 17
Arizona, 29

"Bacchanalian Christmases," 10
Baked ham and maple syrup, 72
Baked stuffed fillets, 72
Baltimore, 70
"Barring out the schoolmaster," 31
Belsnickling, 31
Bible, 11, 15, 23, 31
Big Eating, 37
Bishop Chase of Massachusetts, 18
"Blind Man's Bluff," 61
Boston, 17, 18, 52, 63
Bradford, Governor, 11
Brébeuf, Jean de, 74
Brooks, Phillips, 74

Café Brûlot, 32, 70, 73
California, 36
Calkin, John Baptiste, 74
Call, L. N., 35
Candied cranberries, 73
Carter, Robert, 12
Christmas cards, 63
"Christmas Carol, A," 59
Christmas Day, 9, 12, 17, 28, 29, 52, 59
Christmas decorations, 38-41
Christmas dinner in America, 70
Christmas Eve, 7, 17, 32, 35, 36, 47, 52, 54, 58
Christmas party 11, 35, 43, 44
Christmas service, 9, 12
Christmas tree, 19, 23, 37, 45, 56
"Christmas waits," 37
"Christ was born in Bethlehem and Mary was his niece," 74

Church of England, 11
Civil War, 45
Clark, William, 28
Colonial era, 12, 23
Columbus, Christopher, 9
Continental Army, 7, 17
Cooky pyramid, 22
Corn husk doll, 66-67
Cowboys, 34
Crèche, 32
Creoles, 42
Creole sauce, 72

Delaware River, 10, 17
Delaware River Valley, 31
Dickens, Charles, 59
Donelson, Emily, 44
Donelson, Johnny, 44
Dutch children, 17, 23
Dutch settlers, 18, 70

Eastern Orthodox religion, 37
Eastern seaboard, 22, 31
East Room, 45
Ellipse, 45
England, 13, 16, 18, 45
Enjalran, Father Jean, 22
Epiphany, 22
Eskimos, 37
"Ever-living" tree, 37

Father Christmas, 47
Fir, 14
Firecrackers, 15
Fithian, Philip, 12
Flying Angel, 68
Fremont, John, 28
French trappers, 37
Frontiersmen, 31
Fur trappers, 32

George Washington's eggnog, 15, 70, 71
Georgia, 22, 52
German immigrants, 19
"German Tree," 45
Great Lakes, 32
Great prairies, 35
Great Salt Lake, 35

Hessian troops, 19
Hispaniola, 9
Holiday recipes, 71-73
Holland, 18, 47
Holly, 14, 56
Hopkins, John Henry, Jr., 74
Horsley, John Calcott, 63
Howe, William, 17
"Hunt-the-Slipper," 61
Hurons, 22

"I Heard the Bells on Christmas Day," 74
Indians, 22, 37, 71
Iowa, 35
Iowa River, 35
Irving, Washington, 19
"It Came Upon a Midnight Clear," 58, 74, 75

Jackson, Andrew, 44
James River, 9
Jamestown Colony, 9
Jefferson, Thomas, 12, 23, 28, 44, 71
"Jesus is Born," 74
Jones, Laura, 45
Jones, Major, 52
Jour de l'An, Le, 32
"Joyous fumes of Christmas, The," 15

Kansas, 35
Kentucky mountains, 74
Kissing Day, 37
Kris Kringle, 19, 47
KristKindlein, 19

Lake Huron, 22
Lebkuchen, 22
Lee, Robert E., 29
Lewis, Meriwether, 28
Lincoln, Abraham, 45
Lodgings, The, 36
Longfellow, Henry Wadsworth, 74
Louisiana, 32, 70
Love feast, 22

Mackinac, 74

Madison, Dolley, 44
Maher, Cotton, 12
Manger scene, 22
Massachusetts, 10, 17, 18
Midnight Mass, 22
Mince pie, 11, 15, 18, 70
Minnesota, 35
Mississippi River, 28
Missouri River, 28
Missouri Territory, 32
Mistletoe, 14
Monticello, 23, 71
Moore, Clement, 19, 47
Moravian Christmas cookies, 73
Moravians, 20, 22
Mormons, 35
Mount Vernon, 15, 17, 70
Mummers' Parade, 31

Nativity scene, 22
Navidad colony, 9
Nebraska, 35
New Amsterdam, 18, 23
New England, 17
Newfoundland, 9
New Jersey, 17
New Orleans, 32, 70
New Orleans sweet potato pie, 73
New World, 9, 11, 16, 23, 70
New Year's Day, 32, 70
New Year's Eve, 34
New York City, 18, 54, 55, 56, 70
Noël, 32
Noisemaking, 15
North America, 9, 16
North Carolina, 22, 52
North Dakota, 28
North Pole, 47, 59

"O, Come, All Ye Faithful," 58
Oklahoma Territory, 52
"Old Buck," 52
Old Dominion, 15
Old North Church, 18
"O Little Town of Bethlehem," 74, 77
Ozark Mountains, 52

Papa Noël, 32, 47
Pastores, Los, 36
Pennsylvania, 19, 22, 31
Pennsylvania Avenue, 43
Philadelphia, 31
Puritans, 12, 14, 31
Pierce, Franklin, 45
Pilgrims, 10, 11
Pioneers, 7, 31, 35
Piñata, 37
Plum pudding, 15, 61, 70
Plymouth Colony, 10
Poinsettia, 56
Pomander balls, 69
Posadas, Las, 36
Prang, Louis, 63
Putz, 22

Quakers, 31
Quilted Christmas stockings, 68

Redner, Lewis, 74
Religious services, 7, 15, 35
Réveillon, 32
"Rise Up, Shepherd, and Follow," 74
Roanoke Island, 9
Russians, 37

Sachets, 69
Saint Louis Cathedral, 32
Saint Nicholas, 18, 19, 47
Saint Nicholas Eve, 18
Salt Lake City, 35
Santa Claus, 18, 32, 44, 47, 59
Santa Maria, 9
Santa Fe, 36
Scrooge, Ebenezer, 59
Sears, Edmund H., 74
Shepherds, The, 36
Sinck tuck, 37
Sinterklaas, 18, 47
Sitka, 37
Slaves, 14, 32, 74
Sorrel soup, 71
South Carolina, 29
Spanish-Americans, 36
Spanish influence, 36
Stanton, 28

Texas, 34
Three Wise Men, 32
Town of the Nativity, 9
Traditional American Christmas, 54
Trenton, 19
"'Twas the Night Before Christmas," 61
Twelfth Night, 15, 18

Victoria, Queen, 56
Vikings, 9
Villa de la Navidad, 9
Vimont, Father Barthélémy, 74
Virginia, 9, 12, 13, 14, 15, 18, 29, 45, 70
"Visit from Saint Nicholas, A," 19

Washington, George, 7, 10, 15, 16, 17
Washington, Martha, 15
Wassail bowl, 15, 17
Welles, Gideon, 45
"We Three Kings of Orient Are," 74, 76
Whipple, Amiel, 29
White House, 43, 44, 45
Willis, Richard S., 74
Windsor Castle, 56

Young, Brigham, 35
Yule log, 13, 32
Yuletide, 23, 34, 65

Illustration Acknowledgments

Cover: Nathan Benn, Woodfin Camp, Inc.

2: Smithsonian Institution (Archives of 76, Bay Village, Ohio © J. L. G. Ferris)

8: From *Christmas in Williamsburg*

10: The Museum of Science and Industry, Chicago (World Book photo)

11: The Metropolitan Museum of Art, New York City, Gift of John Stewart Kennedy, 1897

13: (left) The Bettman Archive; (right) Greenfield Village and Henry Ford Museum, Dearborn, Michigan; (below) Picture Collection, The Branch Libraries, The New York Public Library

14: Colonial Williamsburg

16-18: From *Christmas in Williamsburg*

19: Smithsonian Institution (Archives of 76, Bay Village, Ohio © J. L. G. Ferris)

20-21: Bob Scott Studios Inc.

22: Old Salem Restoration, Winston-Salem, North Carolina

24: Shelburne Museum, Vermont

25: Abby Aldrich Rockefeller Folk Art Collection, Williamsburg, Virginia

26: (top right and center) New York Historical Society, New York City; (top left) Abby Aldrich Rockefeller Folk Art Collection, Williamsburg, Virginia; (bottom) Shelburne Museum, Vermont (American Heritage)

27: (top and bottom left) Abby Aldrich Rockefeller Folk Art Collection, Williamsburg, Virginia; (bottom right) Shelburne Museum, Vermont

29: Capitol Building, Helena Montana (Jorud photo)

30: (top) The Harry T. Peters Collection, Museum of The City of New York; (below) Picture Collection, The Branch Libraries, The New York Public Library

32-33: (top) Culver; (bottom) Col. and Mrs. Edgar Garbish Collection (American Heritage)

34: American Heritage

36: Superstock

38: Colonial Williamsburg

39: Colonial Williamsburg; (bottom right) from *Christmas in Williamsburg*

40: Historical Society of Old Newbury, Newburyport, Massachusetts (Time LIFE Books, Time Life Picture Agency)

41: (top) From *Christmas in Williamsburg;* (bottom) Greenfield Village and Henry Ford Museum, Dearborn, Michigan

42-43: Smithsonian Institution (Archives of 76, Bay Village, Ohio © J. L. G. Ferris)

44-45: Paul Wagener

46: Smithsonian Institution

48: Harper's Weekly (American Heritage)

49: (bottom) The New York Historical Society, New York City

50: A Visit from St. Nicholas by Clement C. Moore, LLD. With original cuts designed and engraved by Boyd. Published 1848.

51: Harper's Weekly

53: "Under the Mistletoe" from an engraving dated 1868 (Dover Publications)

54-55: American Heritage

56: Historical Pictures Service

57: Picture Collection, The Branch Libraries, The New York Public Library

58: Library of Congress

59: The New York Public Library Prints Division

60: Greenfield Village and Henry Ford Museum, Dearborn, Michigan

62-64: Hallmark Cards Inc.

65-73: Product Illustration Inc.